MELBOURNE

COLLECTORS WORLD

FLINDERS STREET STATION was built in 1905, on the site from which Australia's first steam train departed in 1854.

MARVELLOUS MELBOURNE." That's what she was known as last century — and the "World's Most Livable City" in more recent times.

Australia's jewel of the south, Melbourne, owes its foundation to John Batman who, in 1835, crossed Bass Strait from Tasmania in search of grazing land. After sailing a few kilometres up the Yarra River from Port Phillip Bay, he stepped ashore declaring "This is the place for a village".

Named after Queen Victoria's Prime Minister in 1836, the plan for a great city was laid out on a grid of spacious boulevards by the surveyor Robert Hoddle the following year.

The proclamation of the new Colony of Victoria in 1851 coincided with the discovery of gold at Bendigo and Ballarat, and Melbourne became the last port of call for tens of thousands of gold seekers convinced they would make their fortunes overnight.

By the time gold had petered out, many of the new settlers had found riches not below

ABOVE:
Bourke Street Mall and the inevitable tram.
LEFT:
A Melbourne moon casts a glistening sheen on
the Rialto, the city's tallest building.
OPPOSITE:
Lunchtime joggers along the tranquility of theYarra
River within walking distance of the city centre.

the ground but on the lush grazing and farming land to the west, north and east of Melbourne.

The wealth created from the gold rush and the land boom of the 1870s and 1880s was reflected in gracious homes, opulent theatres, inspiring churches, expansive parklands and international business houses.

When the Commonwealth of Australia was proclaimed on 1st January, 1901, Melbourne was regarded not only as the new nation's cultural centre, but also its financial capital.

Almost a century on, Melbourne is as charming and dynamic a city as ever. It is, however, a modern city built on proud traditions.

As it has for more than a century, Melbourne (and the nation!) stops for the running of the Melbourne Cup, and it holds its breath on the last Saturday in September when, at the vast Melbourne Cricket ground, where the 1956 Olympic Games opening cer-

LEFT:
Aerial view of the city at night.
RIGHT:
St Paul's Cathedral, built in 1877, boasts the highest Anglican Church spire in the world and Australia's largest bell peel.

was held, 90,000 fanatical supporters gather for a furious sporting contest: the Australian Football League Premiership.

Melburnians love their sport, and the city boasts some of the finest sporting stadiums in the world, as it does some of the finest gardens. Inner Melbourne is lapped by a sea of green and a kaleidoscope of floral colour from the Royal Botanic Gardens, the Alexandra Gardens, the Exhibition Gardens and the Fitzroy Gardens wherein lies Captain Cook's Cottage, the restored English home of Australia's discoverer. These gardens, together with the beaches of Port Phillip Bay and the Yarra River and its tributaries which rise in the blue yonder of the Dandenong Ranges to the east, are the playgrounds and havens for the city's three million people.

A natural haven of another kind is the Royal Melbourne Zoo — the world's third oldest — where exotic animals from all around the globe, as well as Australia's unique koala, kangaroo, wombat and platypus, are cared for in picturesque natural environments. The Healesville Sanctuary, where over 200 species of Australian birds, reptiles and mammals live, and Phillip Island — home of the popular Fairy Penguin — are within two hours of the Zoo, making Melbourne a wonderland for animal lovers.

Melbourne has a distinctive, multi-faceted character. It is a peaceful cosmopolitan city blended from diverse cultural influences. Fine buildings feature a variety of architectural styles of national heritage significance and futuristic symbolism. In the Museum and Library of Victoria and the National Gallery of Victoria, Melbourne houses internationally recognised collections. And in the Victorian Arts Centre and other highly decorative theatres, the city presents theatre, dance and musical productions which attract wide acclaim.

The Shrine of Remembrance stands sentinel to the fallen in the grand tree-lined boulevard of St Kilda Road. Historic Como House and Ripponlea vividly mirror past eras of elegant but staid private living. By contrast, the Victoria Market throngs with the sounds, scents, colours and textures, which reflect the rich polyglot personality of a

ABOVE:
The glittering spire of the Victorian Arts Centre soars above suburban Melbourne, reflecting the city's cultural aspirations.

multi-cultural community. The widest variety of fresh produce imaginable finds its way from the Market onto the tables of the host of quality restaurants that have earnt Melbourne an enviable culinary reputation. Melbourne is unsurpassed in the food and wine it offers: from *haute cuisine* served midst plush decor, to the authenticity of China Town; from the Mediterranean atmosphere of street cafes in Lygon Street, to dining on that very special curiosity, the Melbourne tram.

Celebrations in restaurants and nightclubs spill into the streets at frequent people's festivals and parades which forge a strong community spirit. An example is Melbourne's longest running popular festival, Moomba. This grand parade links the five star hotels, multi-national corporate headquarters and large department stores rising either side of the central business district's leafy thoroughfares with the city's main artery, the Yarra River, where the new Southbank development of fashionable boutiques, galleries and open-air restaurants merges with the arts precinct.

"Marvellous" and "Most Livable": these are two descriptions from different eras that attempt to define Melbourne — a beautiful, vibrant and intriguing city. ■

ABOVE:
King Street, with its restaurants and discotheques, is popular at night.
LEFT:
Gog and Magog, gilded sentinels in the Royal Arcade.

Night view of Crown Casino. Exciting entertainment complex on the banks of the Yarra River.

Above:
View of Melbourne from the Docklands.
Right:
Balloons suspended in the skylit dome of Diamaru, a spectacular Japanese department store in the heart of Melbourne.
Far right:
A gigantic fob watch in Melbourne Central entertains the crowds hourly.

ABOVE LEFT:
Swanston Street Mall, a popular shopping
promenade in the heart of the city.
LEFT:
St Patrick's Cathedral, designed by
William Wardell in 1863, is the largest
cathedral in Australia.
BELOW LEFT:
The State Parliament House, the seat of the
Victorian government. The Commonwealth
Parliament sat here between 1901 and 1927
while Canberra was being developed as
the national capital.

*L*EFT:
*A tranquil sunset on the Yarra as the city's
business district starts turning off the lights.*

*A*BOVE *R*IGHT AND *R*IGHT:
*Melbourne's Chinatown, with its authentic cuisine and
oriental glitter, reflects the city's multi-culturalism, as do
the Victoria Markets, where food producers cater for a
wide variety of ethnic tastes.*

GOVERNMENT HOUSE (*left*) stands adjacent to Melbourne's famous Royal Botanic Gardens. Spread over 42 hectares, the superbly landscaped plantations, flower beds, lawns and ornamental lakes of these gardens provide a lush green refuge in the centre of the city, where busy citizens can enjoy a quiet moment. Many experts regard them the equal of any in the world. The site for the gardens was chosen by Charles Joseph La Trobe in 1845, though expanded and several times since.

The National Herbarium, in the south west corner of the gardens, is of special interest to botanists. A great variety of tropical, sub-tropical and temperate climate flora has been successfully cultivated there. ∎

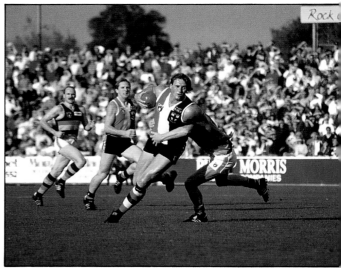

TOP AND OPPOSITE:
The hallowed turf of the Melbourne Cricket Ground, the best known sporting venue in the nation, where crowds of up to 100,000 gather for the city's greatest sporting passions: the AFL Australian Rules Football (see above), and international cricket.
ABOVE LEFT:
Sports crazy Melbourne boasts the most advanced tennis complex in Australia — the National Tennis Centre.
LEFT:
The Melbourne Cup is not only Australia's premier horse race but a cultural institution. Almost the entire nation grinds to a halt during the running of it.

R LIFE
TOWER LI
Energy Wisely
SEC
CLIPSAL
wilco
Vinidex
GET WOOL
WESTERN STAR
WESTERN STAR proudly
Anset

ABOVE:
The Queen Victoria Statue, reflecting the colonial era, dominates the centre of the Domain .
RIGHT:
A promenade along the banks of the Yarra at Southgate, at the edge of the city.

ABOVE:
The broad green sward of Fitzroy Gardens at the
perimeter of the city.
LEFT:
Melbourne has many beautiful Gardens which
are often use for relaxation.

*A*BOVE:
*Westgate Bridge provides access to Melbourne's
western suburbs and Geelong.*
*A*BOVE *L*EFT:
*An aerial view of the city from Albert Park beach on
Port Phillip Bay,which is both a port and a summer
playground for the city.*
*F*AR *L*EFT:
A pelican preens itself in tranquil Hobsons Bay.
*L*EFT:
A view of Melbourne from the Williamstown marina.

OPPOSITE:
The zoo has an excellent collection of big cats,
including the splendid Sumatran tiger.
LEFT:
Though this Australian icon has a grey coat, it is in
fact a female Red kangaroo — with her joey.
ABOVE:
Melbourne Zoo's gardens are beautifully cultivated
and a source of considerable pride for the city.

THE Royal Melbourne Zoological Gardens — better known as the Melbourne Zoo — was the first zoo in Australia and, with a history dating to 1862, is one of the oldest in the world. It offers a glimpse of the beauty and wonder of the natural world, with more than 350 kinds of animals and thousands of plant species. The zoo also plays a significant role in the conservation of threatened species in Australia, co-operating with other regional zoos and wildlife authorities with special breeding programmes. ■

*L*EFT:
*The Shrine of Remembrance, built in 1934 to honour
Australia's many fallen in World War I, now
honours our fallen in all wars.*
*A*BOVE:
*Melbourne's monument to Captain Cook, the great
Royal Navy navigator who started it all with his
voyage of discovery in 1788. His charming English
cottage was transported and re-erected in the city.*

ABOVE:
The Royal Exhibition Building, built for the
International Exhibition of 1880. It was also the
venue for the opening of Australia's
first Federal Parliament.

ABOVE RIGHT:
Como, a legacy of the grand days of the Victorian
"squattocracy", is an architectural blend of
Australian regency and Italianate styles

RIGHT:
The State Library of Victoria and the Museum of
Victoria. The library, built in 1853, is the oldest State
Library in Australia. The museum enjoys an enviable
reputation in its field and is noted for its excellent
Planitarium. The dome, which was added in 1911,
was the largest dome in the world at the time.

ABOVE:
The historic barque, Polly Woodside, was launched in Belfast in 1885. She is one of the few surviving sailing ships of her period.

ABOVE LEFT:
Ripponlea, one of the most elegant surviving 19th Century suburban estates in Australia, was designed in the Romanesque style in the 1860s. The building and gardens remain impressive, despite some Hollywood-style alterations made in the 1930s.

LEFT:
The Princess Theatre, once believed to be haunted by the ghost of the actor Federici, was designed by William Pitt and completed in 1887.

LOOKING across to the city from Southgate.

MELBOURNE is a city that knows how to enjoy
itself, whether dining out, mixing at the wide
variety of cultural gatherings, or cheering at some
of the country's greatest sporting events. But the
annual Mooba Festival is when the citizens all
come together to paint their town crimson.